baby

LOVE

baby

baby

LOVE

baby

Babysitting
COUPON

FOR

1 EVENING OFF

USE IT WISELY! THERE IS A LIMITED NUMBER OF COUPONS AND IT´S STILL 18 YEARS...

DATE: **TIME:**

I WILL ACCEPT CHOCOLATE OR BEER (WHICH I OPEN AFTER RETURNING YOUR BABY!)

baby
LOVE
baby

baby
LOVE
baby

Babysitting

COUPON

FOR

1 EVENING OFF

USE IT WISELY! THERE IS A LIMITED NUMBER OF COUPONS AND IT´S STILL 18 YEARS...

DATE: **TIME:**

I WILL ACCEPT CHOCOLATE OR BEER (WHICH I OPEN AFTER RETURNING YOUR BABY!)

baby

baby

LOVE

LOVE

baby

baby

Babysitting

COUPON

FOR

1 EVENING OFF

USE IT WISELY! THERE IS A LIMITED NUMBER OF COUPONS AND IT'S STILL 18 YEARS...

DATE: **TIME:**

I WILL ACCEPT CHOCOLATE OR BEER (WHICH I OPEN AFTER RETURNING YOUR BABY!)

baby

baby

LOVE

LOVE

baby

baby

Babysitting
COUPON
FOR
1 EVENING OFF

USE IT WISELY! THERE IS A LIMITED NUMBER OF COUPONS AND IT 'S STILL 18 YEARS...

DATE: **TIME:**

I WILL ACCEPT CHOCOLATE OR BEER (WHICH I OPEN AFTER RETURNING YOUR BABY!)

baby

baby

LOVE

LOVE

baby

baby

Babysitting
COUPON
FOR
1 EVENING OFF

USE IT WISELY! THERE IS A LIMITED NUMBER OF COUPONS AND IT 'S STILL 18 YEARS...

DATE: **TIME:**

I WILL ACCEPT CHOCOLATE OR BEER (WHICH I OPEN AFTER RETURNING YOUR BABY!)

Babysitting
COUPON
FOR
1 EVENING OFF

USE IT WISELY! THERE IS A LIMITED NUMBER OF COUPONS AND IT´S STILL 18 YEARS...

DATE: **TIME:**

I WILL ACCEPT CHOCOLATE OR BEER (WHICH I OPEN AFTER RETURNING YOUR BABY!)

baby
LOVE
baby

baby
LOVE
baby

Babysitting

COUPON

FOR

1 EVENING OFF

USE IT WISELY! THERE IS A LIMITED NUMBER OF COUPONS AND IT 'S STILL 18 YEARS...

DATE: **TIME:**

I WILL ACCEPT CHOCOLATE OR BEER (WHICH I OPEN AFTER RETURNING YOUR BABY!)

baby
LOVE
baby

baby
LOVE
baby

Babysitting

COUPON

FOR

1 EVENING OFF

USE IT WISELY! THERE IS A LIMITED NUMBER OF COUPONS AND IT'S STILL 18 YEARS...

DATE: **TIME:**

I WILL ACCEPT CHOCOLATE OR BEER (WHICH I OPEN AFTER RETURNING YOUR BABY!)

baby
LOVE
baby

baby
LOVE
baby

Babysitting
COUPON

FOR

1 EVENING OFF

USE IT WISELY! THERE IS A LIMITED NUMBER OF COUPONS AND IT'S STILL 18 YEARS...

DATE: **TIME:**

I WILL ACCEPT CHOCOLATE OR BEER (WHICH I OPEN AFTER RETURNING YOUR BABY!)

baby
LOVE
baby

baby
LOVE
baby

Babysitting

COUPON

FOR

1 EVENING OFF

USE IT WISELY! THERE IS A LIMITED NUMBER OF COUPONS AND IT'S STILL 18 YEARS...

DATE: **TIME:**

I WILL ACCEPT CHOCOLATE OR BEER (WHICH I OPEN AFTER RETURNING YOUR BABY!)

baby
LOVE
baby

baby
LOVE
baby

Babysitting
COUPON
FOR
1 EVENING OFF

USE IT WISELY! THERE IS A LIMITED NUMBER OF COUPONS AND IT'S STILL 18 YEARS...

DATE: **TIME:**

I WILL ACCEPT CHOCOLATE OR BEER (WHICH I OPEN AFTER RETURNING YOUR BABY!)

baby

baby

LOVE

LOVE

baby

baby

Babysitting

COUPON

FOR

1 EVENING OFF

USE IT WISELY! THERE IS A LIMITED NUMBER OF COUPONS AND IT 'S STILL 18 YEARS...

DATE: **TIME:**

I WILL ACCEPT CHOCOLATE OR BEER (WHICH I OPEN AFTER RETURNING YOUR BABY!)

baby
LOVE
baby

baby
LOVE
baby

Babysitting
COUPON
FOR
1 EVENING OFF

USE IT WISELY! THERE IS A LIMITED NUMBER OF COUPONS AND IT'S STILL 18 YEARS...

DATE: **TIME:**

I WILL ACCEPT CHOCOLATE OR BEER (WHICH I OPEN AFTER RETURNING YOUR BABY!)

baby

baby

LOVE

LOVE

baby

baby

Babysitting

COUPON

FOR

1 EVENING OFF

USE IT WISELY! THERE IS A LIMITED NUMBER OF COUPONS AND IT 'S STILL 18 YEARS...

DATE: **TIME:**

I WILL ACCEPT CHOCOLATE OR BEER (WHICH I OPEN AFTER RETURNING YOUR BABY!)

baby

LOVE

baby

baby

LOVE

baby

Babysitting

COUPON

FOR

1 EVENING OFF

USE IT WISELY! THERE IS A LIMITED NUMBER OF COUPONS AND IT'S STILL 18 YEARS...

DATE: **TIME:**

I WILL ACCEPT CHOCOLATE OR BEER (WHICH I OPEN AFTER RETURNING YOUR BABY!)

baby
LOVE
baby

baby
LOVE
baby

Babysitting
COUPON
FOR
1 EVENING OFF

USE IT WISELY! THERE IS A LIMITED NUMBER OF COUPONS AND IT'S STILL 18 YEARS...

DATE: **TIME:**

I WILL ACCEPT CHOCOLATE OR BEER (WHICH I OPEN AFTER RETURNING YOUR BABY!)

baby

baby

LOVE

LOVE

baby

baby

Babysitting

COUPON

FOR

1 EVENING OFF

USE IT WISELY! THERE IS A LIMITED NUMBER OF COUPONS AND IT'S STILL 18 YEARS...

DATE: **TIME:**

I WILL ACCEPT CHOCOLATE OR BEER (WHICH I OPEN AFTER RETURNING YOUR BABY!)

baby
LOVE
baby

baby
LOVE
baby

Babysitting
COUPON
FOR
1 EVENING OFF

USE IT WISELY! THERE IS A LIMITED NUMBER OF COUPONS AND IT'S STILL 18 YEARS...

DATE: **TIME:**

I WILL ACCEPT CHOCOLATE OR BEER (WHICH I OPEN AFTER RETURNING YOUR BABY!)

baby
LOVE
baby

baby
LOVE
baby

Babysitting

COUPON

FOR

1 EVENING OFF

USE IT WISELY! THERE IS A LIMITED NUMBER OF COUPONS AND IT'S STILL 18 YEARS...

DATE: **TIME:**

I WILL ACCEPT CHOCOLATE OR BEER (WHICH I OPEN AFTER RETURNING YOUR BABY!)

baby

LOVE

baby

baby

LOVE

baby

Babysitting
COUPON
FOR
1 EVENING OFF

USE IT WISELY! THERE IS A LIMITED NUMBER OF COUPONS AND IT'S STILL 18 YEARS...

DATE: **TIME:**

I WILL ACCEPT CHOCOLATE OR BEER (WHICH I OPEN AFTER RETURNING YOUR BABY!)

baby

baby

LOVE

LOVE

baby

baby

Babysitting
COUPON

FOR

1 EVENING OFF

USE IT WISELY! THERE IS A LIMITED NUMBER OF COUPONS AND IT'S STILL 18 YEARS...

DATE: **TIME:**

I WILL ACCEPT CHOCOLATE OR BEER (WHICH I OPEN AFTER RETURNING YOUR BABY!)

baby

LOVE

baby

baby

LOVE

baby

Babysitting

COUPON

FOR

1 EVENING OFF

USE IT WISELY! THERE IS A LIMITED NUMBER OF COUPONS AND IT'S STILL 18 YEARS...

DATE: **TIME:**

I WILL ACCEPT CHOCOLATE OR BEER (WHICH I OPEN AFTER RETURNING YOUR BABY!)

baby
LOVE
baby

baby
LOVE
baby

Babysitting
COUPON
FOR
1 EVENING OFF

USE IT WISELY! THERE IS A LIMITED NUMBER OF COUPONS AND IT'S STILL 18 YEARS...

DATE: **TIME:**

I WILL ACCEPT CHOCOLATE OR BEER (WHICH I OPEN AFTER RETURNING YOUR BABY!)

baby

baby

LOVE

LOVE

baby

baby

Babysitting

COUPON

FOR

1 EVENING OFF

USE IT WISELY! THERE IS A LIMITED NUMBER OF COUPONS AND IT'S STILL 18 YEARS...

DATE: **TIME:**

I WILL ACCEPT CHOCOLATE OR BEER (WHICH I OPEN AFTER RETURNING YOUR BABY!)

baby

baby

LOVE

LOVE

baby

baby

Babysitting

COUPON

FOR

1 EVENING OFF

USE IT WISELY! THERE IS A LIMITED NUMBER OF COUPONS AND IT'S STILL 18 YEARS...

DATE: **TIME:**

I WILL ACCEPT CHOCOLATE OR BEER (WHICH I OPEN AFTER RETURNING YOUR BABY!)

baby

baby

LOVE

LOVE

baby

baby

Babysitting
COUPON
FOR
1 EVENING OFF

USE IT WISELY! THERE IS A LIMITED NUMBER OF COUPONS AND IT'S STILL 18 YEARS...

DATE: **TIME:**

I WILL ACCEPT CHOCOLATE OR BEER (WHICH I OPEN AFTER RETURNING YOUR BABY!)

baby

baby

LOVE

LOVE

baby

baby

Babysitting

COUPON

FOR

1 EVENING OFF

USE IT WISELY! THERE IS A LIMITED NUMBER OF COUPONS AND IT´S STILL 18 YEARS...

DATE: **TIME:**

I WILL ACCEPT CHOCOLATE OR BEER (WHICH I OPEN AFTER RETURNING YOUR BABY!)

baby
LOVE
baby

baby
LOVE
baby

Babysitting
COUPON
FOR
1 EVENING OFF

USE IT WISELY! THERE IS A LIMITED NUMBER OF COUPONS AND IT'S STILL 18 YEARS...

DATE: **TIME:**

I WILL ACCEPT CHOCOLATE OR BEER (WHICH I OPEN AFTER RETURNING YOUR BABY!)

baby

baby

LOVE

LOVE

baby

baby

Babysitting
COUPON
FOR
1 EVENING OFF

USE IT WISELY! THERE IS A LIMITED NUMBER OF COUPONS AND IT´S STILL 18 YEARS...

DATE: **TIME:**

I WILL ACCEPT CHOCOLATE OR BEER (WHICH I OPEN AFTER RETURNING YOUR BABY!)

baby

baby

LOVE

LOVE

baby

baby

Babysitting

COUPON

FOR

1 EVENING OFF

USE IT WISELY! THERE IS A LIMITED NUMBER OF COUPONS AND IT'S STILL 18 YEARS...

DATE: **TIME:**

I WILL ACCEPT CHOCOLATE OR BEER (WHICH I OPEN AFTER RETURNING YOUR BABY!)

baby

LOVE

baby

baby

LOVE

baby

Babysitting

COUPON

FOR

1 EVENING OFF

USE IT WISELY! THERE IS A LIMITED NUMBER OF COUPONS AND IT'S STILL 18 YEARS...

DATE: **TIME:**

I WILL ACCEPT CHOCOLATE OR BEER (WHICH I OPEN AFTER RETURNING YOUR BABY!)

baby

LOVE

baby

baby

LOVE

baby

Babysitting
COUPON
FOR
1 EVENING OFF

USE IT WISELY! THERE IS A LIMITED NUMBER OF COUPONS AND IT´S STILL 18 YEARS...

DATE: **TIME:**

I WILL ACCEPT CHOCOLATE OR BEER (WHICH I OPEN AFTER RETURNING YOUR BABY!)

baby

baby

LOVE

LOVE

baby

baby

Babysitting

COUPON

FOR

1 EVENING OFF

USE IT WISELY! THERE IS A LIMITED NUMBER OF COUPONS AND IT´S STILL 18 YEARS...

DATE: **TIME:**

I WILL ACCEPT CHOCOLATE OR BEER (WHICH I OPEN AFTER RETURNING YOUR BABY!)

baby baby

LOVE LOVE

baby baby

Babysitting

COUPON

FOR

1 EVENING OFF

USE IT WISELY! THERE IS A LIMITED NUMBER OF COUPONS AND IT'S STILL 18 YEARS...

DATE: **TIME:**

I WILL ACCEPT CHOCOLATE OR BEER (WHICH I OPEN AFTER RETURNING YOUR BABY!)

baby

LOVE

baby

baby

LOVE

baby

Babysitting

COUPON

FOR

1 EVENING OFF

USE IT WISELY! THERE IS A LIMITED NUMBER OF COUPONS AND IT'S STILL 18 YEARS...

DATE: **TIME:**

I WILL ACCEPT CHOCOLATE OR BEER (WHICH I OPEN AFTER RETURNING YOUR BABY!)

baby
LOVE
baby

baby
LOVE
baby

Babysitting
COUPON
FOR
1 EVENING OFF

USE IT WISELY! THERE IS A LIMITED NUMBER OF COUPONS AND IT'S STILL 18 YEARS...

DATE: **TIME:**

I WILL ACCEPT CHOCOLATE OR BEER (WHICH I OPEN AFTER RETURNING YOUR BABY!)

baby
LOVE
baby

baby
LOVE
baby

Babysitting

COUPON

FOR

1 EVENING OFF

USE IT WISELY! THERE IS A LIMITED NUMBER OF COUPONS AND IT'S STILL 18 YEARS...

DATE: **TIME:**

I WILL ACCEPT CHOCOLATE OR BEER (WHICH I OPEN AFTER RETURNING YOUR BABY!)

baby
LOVE
baby

baby
LOVE
baby

Babysitting

COUPON

FOR

1 EVENING OFF

USE IT WISELY! THERE IS A LIMITED NUMBER OF COUPONS AND IT'S STILL 18 YEARS...

DATE: **TIME:**

I WILL ACCEPT CHOCOLATE OR BEER (WHICH I OPEN AFTER RETURNING YOUR BABY!)

baby
LOVE
baby

baby
LOVE
baby

Babysitting

COUPON

FOR

1 EVENING OFF

USE IT WISELY! THERE IS A LIMITED NUMBER OF COUPONS AND IT'S STILL 18 YEARS...

DATE: **TIME:**

I WILL ACCEPT CHOCOLATE OR BEER (WHICH I OPEN AFTER RETURNING YOUR BABY!)

baby

baby

LOVE

LOVE

baby

baby

Babysitting
COUPON

FOR

1 EVENING OFF

USE IT WISELY! THERE IS A LIMITED NUMBER OF COUPONS AND IT´S STILL 18 YEARS...

DATE: **TIME:**

I WILL ACCEPT CHOCOLATE OR BEER (WHICH I OPEN AFTER RETURNING YOUR BABY!)

baby
LOVE
baby

baby
LOVE
baby

Babysitting

COUPON

FOR

1 EVENING OFF

USE IT WISELY! THERE IS A LIMITED NUMBER OF COUPONS AND IT'S STILL 18 YEARS...

DATE: **TIME:**

I WILL ACCEPT CHOCOLATE OR BEER (WHICH I OPEN AFTER RETURNING YOUR BABY!)

baby
LOVE
baby

baby
LOVE
baby

Babysitting

COUPON

FOR

1 EVENING OFF

USE IT WISELY! THERE IS A LIMITED NUMBER OF COUPONS AND IT'S STILL 18 YEARS...

DATE: **TIME:**

I WILL ACCEPT CHOCOLATE OR BEER (WHICH I OPEN AFTER RETURNING YOUR BABY!)

baby

LOVE

baby

baby

LOVE

baby

Babysitting

COUPON

FOR

1 EVENING OFF

USE IT WISELY! THERE IS A LIMITED NUMBER OF COUPONS AND IT 'S STILL 18 YEARS...

DATE: **TIME:**

I WILL ACCEPT CHOCOLATE OR BEER (WHICH I OPEN AFTER RETURNING YOUR BABY!)

baby
LOVE
baby

baby
LOVE
baby

Babysitting

COUPON

FOR

1 EVENING OFF

USE IT WISELY! THERE IS A LIMITED NUMBER OF COUPONS AND IT 'S STILL 18 YEARS...

DATE: **TIME:**

I WILL ACCEPT CHOCOLATE OR BEER (WHICH I OPEN AFTER RETURNING YOUR BABY!)

baby
LOVE
baby

baby
LOVE
baby

Babysitting

COUPON

FOR

1 EVENING OFF

USE IT WISELY! THERE IS A LIMITED NUMBER OF COUPONS AND IT'S STILL 18 YEARS...

DATE: **TIME:**

I WILL ACCEPT CHOCOLATE OR BEER (WHICH I OPEN AFTER RETURNING YOUR BABY!)

baby

LOVE

baby

baby

LOVE

baby

Babysitting
COUPON
FOR
1 EVENING OFF

USE IT WISELY! THERE IS A LIMITED NUMBER OF COUPONS AND IT´S STILL 18 YEARS...

DATE: **TIME:**

I WILL ACCEPT CHOCOLATE OR BEER (WHICH I OPEN AFTER RETURNING YOUR BABY!)

baby

LOVE

baby

baby

LOVE

baby

Printed in Great Britain
by Amazon

42326034R00057